Marvel Robinson Jr

Uncaging

Get Out of It

Printed in the United States of America

Published by Marvel Robinson Jr

ISBN: 978-0-578-30228-7

Front and back cover designed through Canva

DEDICATION

This book is dedicated to everyone who feels trapped or caged in. If you're sitting on some talent or ideas, may you find the courage and the faith to overcome your obstacles and share your gift with the world.

May you find something in this book to help you on your journey of uncaging.

PREFACE

After a while you get tired of doubting yourself. You get tired of wasting time, talent and ideas. You get tired of holding yourself back from greatness. At least I did anyway. So, I decided to open up and let my poetry out. I've been writing poetry and rhymes since middle school. The poems in this book date back to 2010 and up to 2021. I finally decided it was time to stop holding them to myself; time to stop caging them in. So, I decided to uncage them to the world, to you. During this process, I shared some of my poetry with family, friends, and co-workers. Their kind words and support helped me complete this book and helped me publish my poetry on YouTube. My goal is to motivate and inspire, so once I put those type of poems in a collection, I was ready. I had to pick myself up and get out of my own way. I had to get out of my head. That's what I mean when I say, 'Get Out of It.' Get out of that trap, that cage. I had to let go and have faith. And it's still a process. I'm still uncaging. But every step forward is a step in the right direction regardless of the shoe size.

MARVEL ROBINSON JR

ACKNOWLEDGMENTS

To my family, friends, followers and supporters, thank you!
To God be the glory

Contents

MAKING HISTORY

From the ground up
we shall make it.
Chances aren't given
so we take it.
A dream is a dream
until we wake it.
Expectations,
we shall break it.

Fears don't run
until you face it.
You know you brave
when you chase it.
Life is better
when you embrace it.
Leave your mark,
they can't erase it.

WHAT IF YOU WERE DREAMING?

What if, what if,
What if you were dreaming?
And all the ideas in your head were screaming,
      "Use me, use me,
      Use me before you wake
      And once this dream is over
      More sense it will make."
Dream big, dream big,
Dream big and find
That everything you dreamt started with your mind.
      Do it, do it,
      And you know what I mean
      Do it as if it were a dream.

REMEMBER YOUR DREAM

Your life is your story
Stick to your theme
To God be the glory
Captain of the team
Don't scurry, don't worry
Build your self-esteem
When life gets blurry
Remember your dream.

DREAM

I close my eyes and paint a picture of what I want to see

And what do I see?

I see everything I want to be

I see everything I want from me

Knowing well it's going to take me to get behind me

So I can get what's mine in front of me

And it's funny because it's right in front of me

But I can't reach it if I keep blocking me

Nobody is stopping me,

But me.

But even with my eyes closed, at least I can see it

My parents told me when I was young

Anything – I can be it

But the one main key, it's up to me to believe it.

So, I'm working on my faith

Trying to pass the test

I see me passing and getting promoted

I feel super blessed

I see me stepping out my way so I can move forward

Then I move forward.

I open my eyes and I see you and me,

Because it's some me in you

It's some fight, it's some love

You got dreams too

I hope you fight for what you love

I hope your dreams come true

And I hope your faith is strong

So you'll know when to step aside

and let the spirit carry you.

FOCUS

Focus, I must stay
On the grind every day
I'm trying to shine in every way
To make them proud until I lay.

I have to shine just like the light
I'll find a way just give me sight
Through the rough, deep dark night
Will focus keep me alright?

I'm alright, I must admit
Come too far so why quit
God on my side so that's who I'm with
Put God first and don't forget.

MOTIVATION

Motivation is what I want

Motivation is what I need

If motivation was life,

Then motivation I breathe.

If only I had it,

Then I wouldn't have to grab it

On a road by itself

Just riding, no traffic.

Motivation can drive you

Just sit back and ride

It will take you somewhere

And show you deep down inside

That you had it in you

A message it sent you

That you can do whatever

There is no need to pretend to.

With motivation you do you
With motivation you do your best
Just do your thing
And don't worry about the rest.

With motivation you stand tall
With motivation you ball
I wrote this poem with motivation
I guess I had it after all.

BETTER THAN BEST

Good ain't good enough
     And your best ain't really your best
You can always do better
     Put yourself to the test
It's plenty time to sleep
     At the end is when you rest
But until then,
     Do better than your best.

I CAN

Practice
what you know.
Learn
what you don't.
Two feet,
you have to stand.
Turn I can't
into I can.

LIKE THE SUN

Anybody can do anything
I hope somebody do something.
Just because everybody can't do everything
Doesn't mean you just do nothing.

Get off the grass and get some cash
You have to walk before you run.
If you fall down, get back up
And rise like the sun.

GROW THROUGH

Staring in a daze
Stuck in his ways
This man's name is Joe

He says life is a maze
He's at this phase
Where he's too scared to go

His friend named Ted
Is wise in the head
And now Joe wants to know

How to get ahead
So Ted said,
"Like a tree, you gotta grow."

NEXT LEVEL SATISFACTION

The so-called perfect people make mistakes
Which means nobody is perfect
There are people who will do whatever it takes
If they feel whatever is worth it

The next step may be the hardest to take
Because it's new and unsure
But if you're sick and tired of the ache
Up ahead is the cure.

BETTER YOURSELF

Superman, superwoman, you know who you are
You belong in the sky, you're a star.

On the road to success, you'll go far
But everybody can't ride in your car.

Know your team, know your sport, play your position
Play to win; this game is not an exhibition.

Blood, sweat, and tears, may they pour with ambition
You are your biggest competition.

CLIMBING MOUNTAINS

Shackles on our mind not our feet
Still trying to find a way to be free
Set the system up against us they had to cheat
Feeling locked out all along we were the key

Voices ain't heard but we still speak
Justice ain't served but we still seek
Climbing mountains in hope to reach the peak
Together strong, divided weak.

UNITED

My motivation is for the both of us
Not just some of us but all of us.
Victory for one of us
Is victory for the rest of us.
There's hope for us
And more for us
That's waiting on us
Just wait on us.
Success is at the door, welcoming us
Thank you, failure, for strengthening us.

THANKS FOR THE REMINDER

Shout out to change for reminding me I'm versatile.
Shout out to challenges for reminding I'm able.
Shout out to worry for reminding me I'm optimistic.
Shout out to doubt for reminding me I'm confident.

Shout out to fear for reminding me I'm brave.
Shout out to hate for reminding me I'm loved.
Shout out to failure for reminding me I'm trying.
Shout out to pain for reminding me I'm strong.

DEEP IN THE CORE

The struggle is real
The kneels kneeled
Down on the floor

Missing a meal
The stomach squealed
Desperate for a store

It's hard to feel
When the heart's concealed
On the sleeve it has been tore

The pain will heal
Strength revealed
Greatness deep in the core

WHEN LIFE HITS

On his back, on the mat, he lay
But down he refuses to stay
Even when down he still looks up
His glass is a half full cup
Some say it's just his luck
And when life swung, they say he should've duck
This man is down, but he is not out
And around him he can hear the doubt
"Stay down, you can't win
If you get back up, you'll get knocked down again"
And even if it's true he doesn't accept it
Quit – he'll do anything except it
Something just came over his spirit
Life – he no longer fears it
He's on his way up and everyone feels it
"You can do it!" now everyone cheers it
He's found the courage and the strength to stand up
And he proceeds to put his hands up
He gets right back into his stance
And tells life let's continue this dance
He knows life will hit him, he can take it
It's the punches that he takes that help him make it
He's a fighter; he has heart and its showing
Through the blood, sweat, and tears he keeps going.

NO PAIN, NO GAIN

The truth hurts, lies help ease the pain
The pain, without it there is no gain

Lose to win, winning brings you fame
At the top, you will realize it's all game

The sooner you play the better, don't mind the weather
Whether sunny or rainy, keep your umbrella

Be brave, sometimes you have to be **bold**
Dig a little deeper, don't worry you'll find your gold.

GO FOR MINE

They say let it be
Everything will be fine
Through my eyes it's hard to see
Steady searching for a sign
    Somebody spilled the tea
    They've been drinking too much wine
    Their words stung me like a bee
    Stuck with me like a porcupine

They were so happy and so free
Two things that seems hard to find
It's something that they told me
Something that was on their mind
They said,
    "Life is like a sea
    Search for fish and fish you find
    What's yours is yours and not for me
    That's why I had to go for mine."

SHOOT TO THE SKY

They say you will never know until you try
"You can't do it" is the biggest lie
Although some goals seem really high
Keep shooting to the sky.

BEGINNING TO GLOW

In the sky, with the birds, with the planes
In the air, I smile, I sang
Up high with the clouds, with the moon
I am a star; I'm due to shine pretty soon.

MOONLIGHT TO SUNSHINE

If the goal is in the sky,
Then I shoot to the cloud
Watch my shot go through
The thunder's my crowd,
Roaring loud.
At night the sky screams,
"I'm black and I'm proud!"

And I smile.

Even against the odds,
Let's grind.
In our darkest moments
We find a way to shine.
We are the stars
In the eyes of the moon
And the sun's coming soon.

PATIENCE

Tick-tock tick-clock
Here comes the chime
Pray for it, wait for it
It just takes time.

PATIENCE AND WAITING

Patience,
Waiting for time
But time is not waiting
Spending time with no money
How much are you paying
Attention,
Listen
The sum can make a difference
But to some
The sum
Defines their existence
Existing thoughts are waiting to be existent
Goals and girls are both waiting for commitment
Dedication
Decisions
They need my attention
But choices don't always show your real intention
Expectations are showing
So, I'm at the movies
I'm face to face with the mirror
Like let's do this
Because all the time I wasted now
Is useless

If I keep waiting for a hint
I'll end up clueless.

But patience,
Patience and waiting are two tricky things
One brings you roses
And the other brings you chicken wings
Enjoy the season
Enjoy the smell
Enjoy the taste
Whatever it is you're after
Take your shot
Enjoy the chase.

LOST TIME IS NEVER FOUND

Make the most of life
Don't waste your time sitting around
Live and love your life
Because lost time is never found.

Time is moving fast
But you have to keep up
Can't let the time past,
I think it's time to step up.

You can do anything
For you are somebody
Plus, you mean everything
You're a special somebody.

But time is not going to wait
It is going to steady move
Just don't lose your fate
You still have more to prove.

EMOTIONS

Sometimes you're happy
Sometimes you're mad
At times you feel good
At times you feel bad

There are many emotions
So many to name
Have you feeling one way
But that can easily change

When you get too happy
People try to bring you down
They'll say you smile too much
Like they rather see you frown

When you get too mad
You do things that day
Things that you regret
Like scaring the people you love away

Then when you get too sad
People ask, "what's wrong?"
You get tired of answering
Because you want to be alone

So don't let everyone see your emotions
If you do, you will regret
Don't get too happy, too mad or too sad
Just stay cool, calm and collect.

HIDE AND SMILE

Hiding his frustrations with a smile
And he's been smiling for a while
Is that really a happy child?

Putting all his worries in a bag
And marking it red flag
Yet, still letting it drag

Patience is trying to walk out the door
She can't wait with him no more
Emotions are starting to pour

But crying has never been in style
Haven't shed a tear in a while
Hiding his frustrations with a smile.

PUSH ON

Your biggest disguise is your smile,
    you wear it well.
You haven't worn it in a while,
    and I can tell.
From far away let's say a mile,
    I can smell.
All the crap cramping your style,
    make you want to yell.

But don't fold, up ahead
    just keep on looking.
The only one in the kitchen,
    but keep on cooking.
When it's over may you rest
    on the best cushion.
Until then, like a car with no gas,
    just keep on pushing.

LIFELINE

When the eyes can't see,
what gives you sight?

When it's dark and no power,
what gives you light?

When you feel like dying,
don't flirt with a knife.

Turn to the one who gives you life.

HOW CAN I HELP?

I see you on the ground in the dirt
I can tell you're in pain and it hurt
You have stains of failure all in your shirt
It seems like everything you try doesn't really work.

I brought positive energy and poured help in a cup
Drink it; dust yourself off, while you get up
No longer do you have to feel stuck
I am here to help and to be your streak of luck.

PAPER THOUHGTS

Grab a pen or pencil,
whichever you prefer.
Place it on me
until words begin to occur.
Don't stop at words,
bring your feelings too.
And you don't have to worry
about me judging you.

I've been waiting for you to speak,
tell me what's on your mind.
You have a story to tell, and I will listen,
I have nothing but time.
Tell me a secret if you like,
I won't tell.
Come to me and be free,
leave your cell.

YOU MATTER

What they think
> Doesn't matter

What they say
> Doesn't matter

Who are they?
> Doesn't matter

Just be you,
> Because you matter.

ALONE VS LONELY

Just because someone is alone
It doesn't mean their lonely.

Someone can feel lonely
and not be alone.
The people around them could be so phony
That they indeed wish
they were actually alone.

Someone can be by themselves
and have the most fun
Compared to someone in a group
where the love is numb.

How long will you be alone
before you become lonely?

And even if you are lonely
you're not alone,
because you're not the only.

RIVER OF TEARS

The wind made her shiver,
What a blow
Feeling sick to her liver,
Feeling low
If somewhere the lining is silver,
Let is show
Because when she looks in the mirror,
She just doesn't know.

Lost is she, so nearer
I walk slow
The pain is clearer
The streams await to flow
Had nothing to give her
But a helping hand might help her row
I told her take me to your river,
I want to go.

TAKE THIS

The advice we give can be the hardest to take
Is that the reason why we give it away?
Some of the best meals take the longest to make
But if you want it bad enough, you will wait.

Be patient.

Treasure is found on the edge of giving up
Don't jump off when it gets tough.
Think of time being in a cup
Be careful when you sip it, you've waste enough.

Be direct.

Make your bed and your mind up
So, when you sleep, you'll be at peace.
Sooner or later, it will be time up
I just hope to see your smile increase.

Be happy.

WATER IS GONNA WATER

We're still going to have fun
Even though there's no sun
Just because one drops
Doesn't mean we all have to run.

Don't hang your head low
When the lights green you have to go
This is my stage
And the rain won't stop this show.

STOMPING IN THE RAIN

Stomping in the rain
But it's not because I'm mad
And it's not because if you asked how my day was, I'd
say bad.

I'm stomping in the rain
But it's not because I'm sad
And it's not because of an umbrella that I wish I had.

Stomping in the rain
In the sky there is a flash
No time soon will this rain be slowing.

I'm stomping in the rain
It makes the water splash
It keeps me entertained until I get where I'm going.

INSPIRED BY THE RAIN

No T.V., no music
All I hear is rain
No swerving, no getting over
I'm in my own lane
What don't kill me makes me stronger
No pain, no gain
Hard, but sweet
Life's like a candy cane.

ENERGY

The sun don't shine until you smile
When you cry, outside it starts to rain
If you're mad, then here comes the thunder
When you're hurting, I too am in pain.

I feel everything you feel
Because we are one and the same
The world moves off your energy
Your energy controls the game.

LET GO

Sitting
Thinking
What's next?
Where do I go from here?
Sometimes my thoughts are dark cloudy
Wish they were sunny clear
I try to plan things out
The wheel I try to steer
Maybe I should let go
Let go of fear.

Fear of going the wrong way
Fear of turning
Fear of making a mistake
But that's called learning
Courage
Bravery
Fearlessness is what I'm yearning
See the smoke
Smell the smoke
My fears are burning.

The more I add the flames get higher

Who am I kidding; I'm afraid of that fire.
The same fire I started I want to put out
I'm thinking about running I got my foot out.

But hold on I'll stay strong
Patiently waiting this might take long

Longer than I thought
And if fear is just a thought
How come I can't just think it away?
It remains it stays
If it leaves it will be back next day
Like come on come out and play
And what I'll say,
Sorry not today,
Go back to bed and lay
I can't live that way.

So here I am trying to fight back tears
Trying to face my fears
Trying to gain back years
That I lost to fear
I'm close, I'm near
Said I'm close, I'm near.

WHAT WOULD YOU DO IF YOU WEREN'T AFRAID? (ASK YOURSELF)

Dark is the sky at night
The opposite of stars which are bright
Like them I hope to rise and shine
But right now, it is something bothering my mind

The sounds I hear seem near
And closer and closer comes fear
He is sneaky as a creeper in a house
And moves quick like the creature is a mouse

He will make you scream like the one who wears the mask
What would you do if you weren't afraid is what I ask?

      Stand up to fear.

I do it and he slowly goes away
Faced it with courage and now I feel okay.

IT'S OKAY

(I tell myself)
It's okay to feel afraid
But don't let that fear think it's okay to stay
My mind I try to persuade
Fear in the passenger seat as I try to drive it away
Convincing myself that I'm brave
That's the only way to make it through the day
Don't want to take fear to the grave
Unless I'm dropping it off and going about my way

It's okay to let go
Hurting myself by holding on
Real feelings don't show
And a life doesn't last that long
Water helps you grow
So tears get pass along
The healing is slow
But you come out feeling strong

It's okay to shine your light
It's helping others see
The stars come out at night
As if their finally free

Stand tall and reach your height
A tree is going to be a tree
If the battle is worth the fight
Then sting like a bee

It's okay to stand out
In a room full of seats, I rather stand up
Things don't always pan out
But that doesn't mean you give your plan up
There's enough success to hand out
That's why I got my hand up
And when fear ran out
It was because my faith ran up.

DANCING WITH OPPORTUNITY

When opportunity asks for your hand
Don't be shy, don't be bland
Give opportunity a chance
And at least one dance.

FLY

Fly, fly, fly away
Enjoy the wings you have today
Tomorrow someone else will fly
I hope to see you in the sky.

I HEARD A BIRD

I was up when the first bird started singing
Wishing I knew the language so I could know the
meaning
And I was up before the phone started ringing
Dirty like a bird we could both use some cleaning

Despite my flaws I'm graced by the sun
With the birds singing today should be fun
With this energy I might go for a run
With no one to race, the early bird already won

One thing I noticed; the bird sung before it flew
Was it a wake-up song to everyone or just the one's it
knew?
I'm up like the early bird, but what should I do?
Then it hit me, let me use my voice and thank the Lord
too

Because if a Robin can say thank you then so can I
It is a blessing to be here and see the sky
So instead of running, today I will fly
And spread the wings that was given to me from the
most high.

REGARDLESS

I hope you reach the place
Where you look hate in the face
And say you can continue your race
But I love you, regardless.

I hope when fear arrives
You don't run and try to hide
Nor step aside and let it inside
But stand and be brave, regardless.

I hope whatever stress and anxiety you sense
Wash away when you rinse
Loosen up when you're tense
So you can relax, regardless.

I hope your losses don't leave you defeated
Nor your mistakes become repeated
But hope your doubt gets deleted
So you can win, regardless.

WEAR YOUR CROWN

Wear your crown queen, wear your crown
Hold it down queen, hold it down
Look around queen, you're blessing the town
Wear your crown queen, wear your crown

Wear your crown king, wear your crown
Off the ground king, off the ground
They can't hold you down king, they can't hold you down
Wear your crown king, wear your crown

We can't let the outside inside, it'll tear us down
Somethings are destined and greatness is something I know I'm bound
Amazing grace I once was lost but now I'm found
Along with my crown

Wear yours!

CHERISH THE PRESENT

In a room
with the lights off
that is when he reaches his deepest thoughts.
Staring at a pitch-black ceiling
with the same color walls
it is so easy to get lost.

Remembering the old days
unwrapping the past like a present.
And still hoping for better days
as he is stuck in the present.

But where there is a lesson to be learned
there is a lesson to be taught.
The present is a gift
 that simply can't be bought.

BUILD ON IT

Turn the page and there's a blank one,
waiting to be filled.
New hopes, new opportunities,
waiting to be revealed.

I hope you're ready because there's a deal,
waiting to be sealed.
So, open your eyes ladies and gentlemen,
we have a new day to build.

START TODAY

Oh, but you can change in a day
    No need to wait for a year
Listen to me when I say
    Don't be held back by fear
The bad habits, the old way
    From them you shall veer
Better habits come out and play
    And now it's sunny and clear
The storm has gone away
    And now success is near
Get on the freeway
    Keep straight from here
I say you can change in a day
    Just stay focus all year
Don't forget what I say
    Don't be held back by fear.

TODAY

Yesterday
is gone.
Tomorrow
hasn't been born.
Today
is the only day
we live.

TOMORROW CAME AND SAID

Oh, you thought you had tomorrow until tomorrow
came and said,

      "Nah, we are going a different route today
      You should've done that yesterday
      You should've, would've, could've but your
      chances went away
      And I may give it back or I may get in the way
      Because the plans I got for you just might take
      all day

      And I see your little attitude, don't be mad at me
      okay
      You should show a little gratitude, and be
      thankful for today
      But you rather turn your back on me, the
      definition of betray
      You still caught up in the past homey, trying to
      conquer yesterday

      So now you are playing catch up, trying to pick
      up where you left off

But to me that's like a slap in the face, you are
telling me to step off
It's not my fault that yesterday your goals didn't
get checked off
Today, I'm your primary concern; I'm where
you should've led off

And forgive me for being emotional; I just
didn't think I was going to make it
They always say, 'tomorrow ain't promised,'
they didn't even think I was going to make it

So yeah, I'm desperate for your attention, don't
put me off my friend."

Stop thinking you got tomorrow when today could be
the end.

ABOUT THE AUTHOR

Marvel Robinson Jr is a writer who focuses on motivating his readers. His personal journals, quotes, and poetry have transitioned to him writing books like "Go for It: Believe You Can Achieve," and "Uncaging: Get Out of It." He graduated from Jacksonville State University with a bachelor's degree in Journalism. After not getting a full-time job in his field right away, he found the extra time and motivation to write. He has a passion for writing and motivating others. He loves to see the results of getting through to someone.

For more from this author visit:
Website: amazon.com/author/marvelrobinsonjr

YouTube: @MarvelRobinson

www.ingramcontent.com/pod-product-compliance
Lightning Source LLC
Chambersburg PA
CBHW030826060726
47590CB00004B/1416